Checks and Balances

PRESS FREEDOM AND AN INDEPENDENT JUDICIARY

RULE OF LAW
EDUCATION CENTRE

Material written by Alex McDermott, with the assistance of the team at the Rule of Law Education Centre: Sally Layson, Justine Hanks, Aaron Martano, Miranda Stewart and Jessica Speed.

Published in 2024 by Connor Court Publishing Pty Ltd

Copyright © Rule of Law Education Centre

www.ruleoflaw.org.au

All rights reserved. No part of this book may be reproduced or transmitted in any form or by any means, electronic or mechanical, including photo copying, recording or by any information storage and retrieval system, without prior permission in writing from the publisher.

Connor Court Publishing Pty Ltd
PO Box 7257
Redland Bay QLD 4165

sales@connorcourt.com.au | www.connorcourt.com

Phone 0497 900 685

Printed in Australia
ISBN: 9781923224179

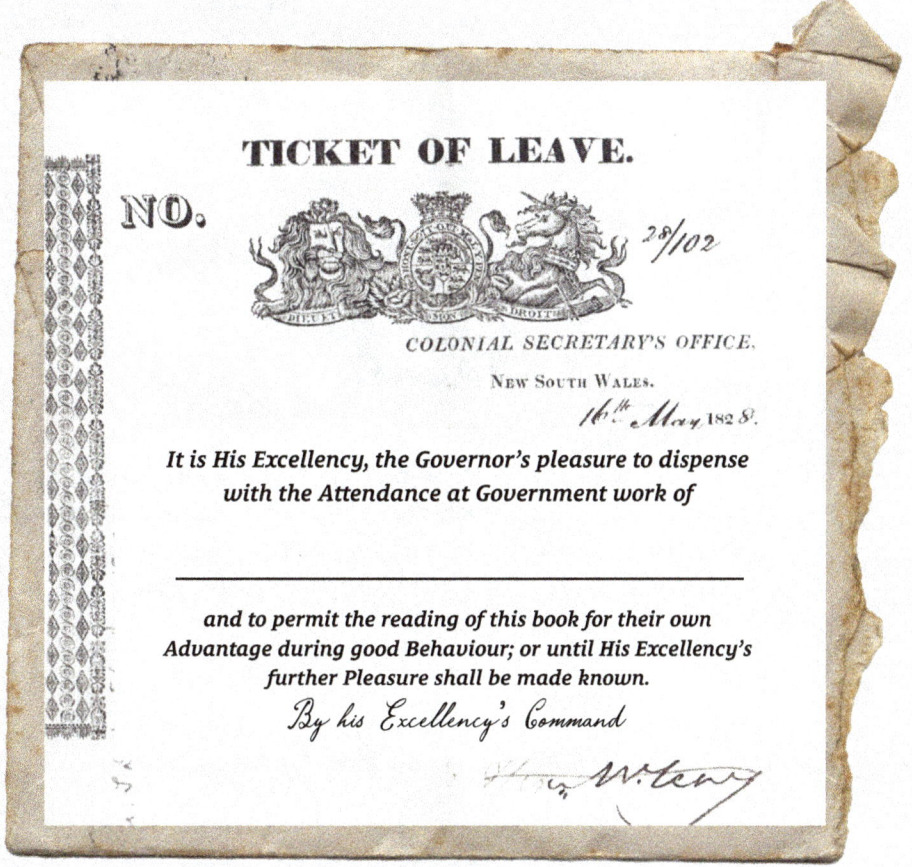

— *Dedication* —

This book is dedicated to the countless judges in Australia who work tirelessly
to provide justice, and who uphold the belief of Chief Justice Forbes that
"the judicial office itself stands uncontrolled and independent,
and bowing to no power but the supremacy of the law."

Checks and Balances

PRESS FREEDOM AND AN INDEPENDENT JUDICIARY

How the establishment of the Supreme Court of New South Wales and a free press provided essential checks on the power of the Governor.

Background to the Story: The Bigge Reports*

Commissioner John Thomas Bigge was sent to the colony of New South Wales in 1819 to report on the state of the settlements.

He was instructed to make recommendations based upon the assumption that the settlement was a place of punishment and reformation and a receptacle for offenders where transportation should invoke real terror.

In 1822 and 1823 he released 3 reports known as the Bigge Reports.

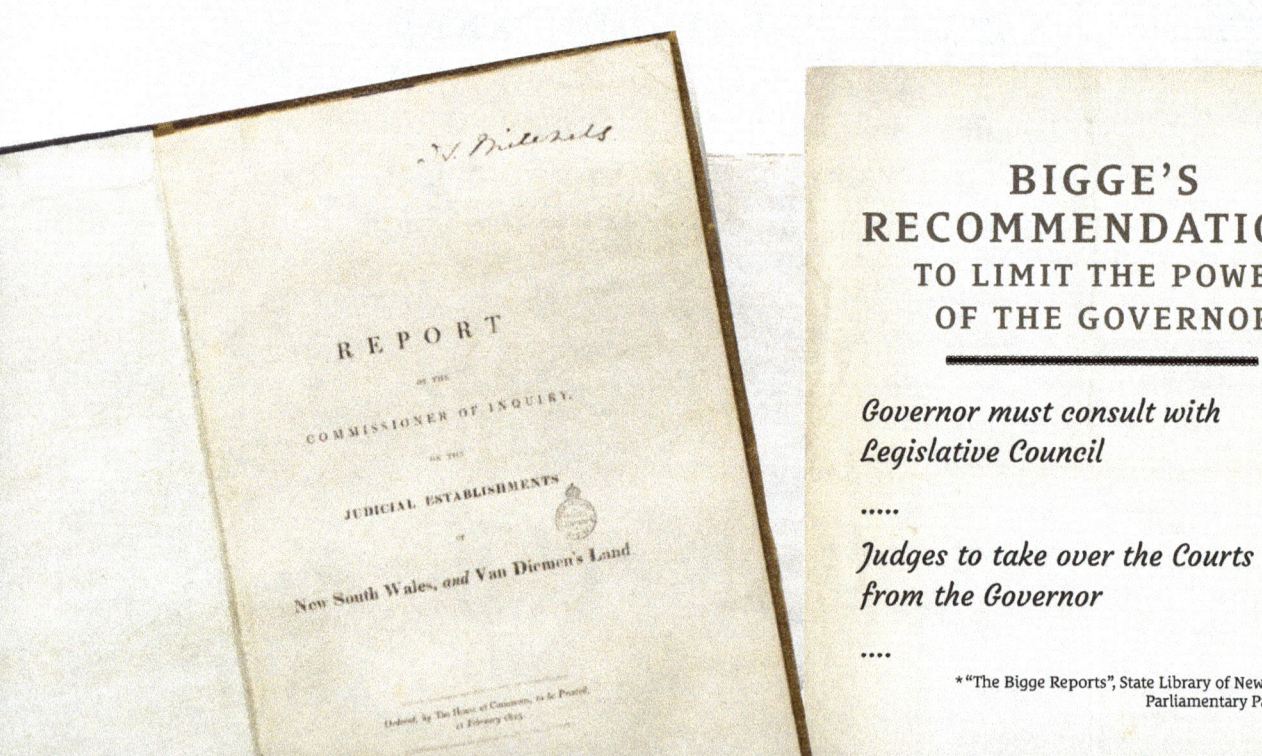

BIGGE'S RECOMMENDATIONS TO LIMIT THE POWER OF THE GOVERNOR

Governor must consult with Legislative Council

.....

Judges to take over the Courts from the Governor

....

*"The Bigge Reports", State Library of New South Wales, Parliamentary Paper 33, 1823.

Timeline

1788
First Fleet arrived. The British colony of New South Wales established as a penal colony.

1822/23
New South Wales Act written in response to the Bigge Report. The New South Wales Act established the NSW Supreme Court.

1824
Francis Forbes arrived in New South Wales as the first Chief Justice of the NSW Supreme Court.
'The Australian' newspaper founded.

1825
Governor Ralph Darling arrived in New South Wales.

1826
Darling portrayed as a tyrant by 'The Australian' as a former soldier dies while serving a harsh sentence that Darling himself had given.

1827
Darling attempted to limit the freedom of the press through two Bills. Forbes refuses to approve the Bills and the matter is sent to Britain for a decision.

1828
The British Government decided that Forbes was correct in preventing Darling's actions and protecting the rights of the citizens of the colony.

It is December 1825 and the new Governor has just arrived on the shores of New South Wales' British colony.

He brings a strong and clear set of instructions from the British government.

The Governor is a military man. Ralph Darling is his name.

He is good at giving commands and having people follow, and by the looks of the state of the colony, there will be lots of orders and instructions to give.

INSTRUCTIONS*

Get tough on convicts.

.....

Pull the colony into shape.

....

*"Earl Bathurst to Governor Darling", 12 July 1825, *Historical Records of Australia*, Series 1, Vol 12, page. 16 (June 1825-1826).

The colony has been left to its own devices for a lot of the time since its establishment in 1788. Although it was established as a penal colony for sentenced criminals, New South Wales is far from being managed like a prison.

Instead, it is run as an open and free society, which just happens to be populated by convicts, ex-convicts and free settlers.

Most convicts are allowed to live on their own and many even start their own families within the colony. Convicts have a lot of free time and often run their own businesses. Their work is often finished by midday, leaving them free to do what they want. If they are skilled workers they are often allowed to go completely free – given 'tickets-of-leave' – very soon after their arrival.

There are convict lawyers, architects, builders, carpenters, surveyors, doctors, teachers and tutors. The streets of Sydney are filled with shops and yards owned and run by convicts and ex-convicts.

Walking down the streets you would find it difficult to tell who was a convict, and who was free.

The British government has decided that this is not a good look. New South Wales does not seem to be working as a place of punishment. Instead, it is looking more and more like a chance for convicts to start again in life.

There are even rumours that criminals in London are deliberately trying to get transported to Australia.

No, this will not do at all.

The British government decides that something must change. They must turn New South Wales into a proper penal colony.

PRIORITIES
FOR THE NSW COLONY

Make people in London so afraid of being transported that they obey the law

...

Tougher restrictions on convicted criminals

...

Stop rewarding convicts by letting them work and run their own business

...

Hold central criminal records for each convict

...

And they think that army man Ralph Darling is just the fellow to help them do this.

Darling is brilliant at working in military hierarchies, where everyone has to follow orders. He thinks that being Governor of a convict colony is like commanding an army. He expects each convict to submit to his authority and to obey his every word.

In the early days of the New South Wales colony, the Governor is the fountain head of authority, and he has powers more sweeping than in any other British colony.

The convicts might have plenty of personal freedom, but the Governor's word often has the effect of law.

The only official check on his power is the British Government, and they are all the way on the other side of the world. It takes more than a year for any mail to get a reply.

This is not much of a check.

The colony to which Darling is arriving is changing, and not just because the British government wants to convert it into a place of salutary terror.

Thanks to the 1823 NSW Act, passed by the British Parliament, things are starting to change.

NEW SOUTH WALES ACT 1823 (UK)

Where it is expedient ...

to erect and establish courts of judicature in NSW ... which shall be styled the Supreme Court of NSW

...

appoint a council ... and with the advice of the council... to make laws and ordinances for the peace welfare and good government of the said colony

...

and Chief Justice of Supreme Court shall have transmitted to Governor ... a certificate ... that such proposed law is not repugnant to the laws of England but is consistent with such laws so far as the circumstances of the said colony will admit

* "New South Wales Act 1823", 4 Geo. IV C. 96, House of Lords Record Office.

The 1823 NSW Act responds to the
Bigge Report recommendations.

For the first time in the colony, there will be separation of powers, and effective checks and balances on those in power.

Now, there will be a Legislative Assembly, and an Executive Council, which the Governor must now consult.

Additionally, there is the newly created Supreme Court.

The Supreme Court's job is to administer justice according to the law. The Governor can no longer control the courts.

Instead, the Chief Justice will ensure that the Governor's actions are lawful, and that any laws the Governor himself creates are within his powers.

The man at the head of the Supreme Court is the same person who helped write the 1823 NSW Act. He takes justice and the law incredibly seriously.

His name is Francis Forbes.

Francis Forbes is a child of the law as much as Darling is a product of the army. He moved to London to study law whilst he was a teenager and brought to the colony 500 legal books for his personal library.

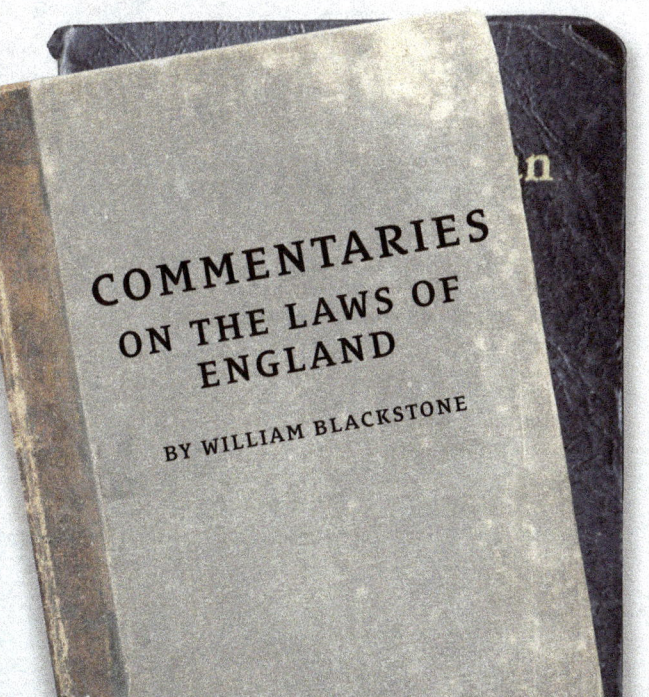

Forbes has a strong admiration for the idea of freedom, and the way the rule of law with an independent judiciary protects those freedoms.

INSTRUCTIONS*

Get tough on convicts.

.....

Pull the colony into shape.

....

Forbes supports the instructions which the British government has given Darling, to organise the colony and keep order amongst the convicts.

But he is also determined to remain faithful to the spirit of the 1823 NSW Act, which has created new institutions such as the Supreme Court. As the Chief Justice of the Supreme Court, Forbes' role is to be a check on the Governor's power and to protect the freedoms of those in the colony.

NEW SOUTH WALES ACT 1823 (UK)

Where it is expedient ...

to erect and establish courts of judicature in NSW ... which shall be styled the Supreme Court of NSW

...

appoint a council ... and with the advice of the council ... to make laws and ordinances for the peace welfare and good government of the said colony

...

and Chief Justice of Supreme Court shall have transmitted to Governor ... a certificate ... that such proposed law is not repugnant to the laws of England but is consistent with such laws so far as the circumstances of the said colony will admit

*"Earl Bathurst to Governor Darling", 12 March 1826, *Historical Records of Australia*, Series 1, Vol 12, page. 219 (June 1825-1826).
"New South Wales Act 1823", 4 Geo. IV C.96, House of Lords Record Office.

However, Forbes and the Supreme Court are not the only checks on the Governor's power about which Darling has to worry.

A year before his arrival, there had begun the experiment of a free press in the colony.

Originally the colony had just one newspaper, the Sydney Gazette, which published the Governor's proclamations and instructions as well as bits of news. You could hardly consider it 'freedom of the press' if it could only write positive comments on the administration of the colonial government.

The Sydney Gazette

NEWS FOR TODAY — 15 APRIL 1824

PROCLAMATION FROM GOVERNOR BRISBANE:

"His Majesty hath been graciously pleased … to establish a Court of Judicature in the Colony… and to appoint FRANCIS FORBES, Esquire, Barrister at Law, to be the CHIEF JUSTICE of the said Court."

---

*"Proclamation by His Excellency Sir Thomas Brisbane." 15 April 1824, *The Sydney Gazette and New South Wales Advertiser.*

This changed in 1824, when a young man named William Wentworth returned from England, where he had been studying at university to become a lawyer.

He arrived back in New South Wales with a printing press and good friend and fellow lawyer, Robert Wardell.

Without even asking the Governor's permission, in October 1824, the two began their own newspaper.

They called it The Australian*, and used it to debate and criticise public issues, including actions of the government with which they disagreed.

In the opening editorial they proclaimed:

> # The Australian
>
> **NEWS FOR TODAY** 14 October 1824
>
> A free press is the most legitimate, and, at the same time, the most powerful weapon that can be employed to annihilate influence, frustrate the designs of tyranny, and restrain the arm of oppression.*

The British government, however, thought that a free press in a colony of convicts was foolish:

"The entire exemption of the Publishers from all restraint of the Local Government must be highly dangerous in a Society of so peculiar a description"...*

* The Australian newspaper published in 1824 is different from the current Australian newspaper which was first published in 1964 by Rupert Murdoch.
The Australian (NSW:1824-1848), 14 October 1824, page. 2
"Earl Bathurst to Governor Darling", 12 July 1825, *Historical Records of Australia*, Series 1, Vol 12, page. 16 (June 1825-1826).

And so, a new idea was embodied in Governor Darling's instructions.

There would now be an annual licence which each newspaper needed in order to be published.

To get the licence, one had to apply to the Governor.

The licence would be cancelled if the publisher, the printer or the proprietor were convicted of publishing any defamatory material which damaged the reputation of people without good cause. Also, the licence could be cancelled if the Governor, with the advice of his Executive Council, decided to.

INSTRUCTIONS

*PART 2**

Annual Licence fee approved by the Governor

....

This means that the Governor has the complete discretion to choose who is licensed to publish a newspaper and would be free to remove their licence at any time.

*"Earl Bathurst to Governor Darling", 12 July 1825, Historical Records of Australia, Series 1, Vol 12 (June 1825-1826)

Even though the British government instructs Governor Darling to implement the press licensing law, he initially holds off.

He knows there will be trouble if he introduces such a harsh clamp on the press. He also knows that Chief Justice Forbes has strong doubts about allowing this law to be implemented.

Even in a colony populated by convicts, Forbes thinks the press should not be under the control of the Governor.

He sees the proposed licensing system as a restriction on free speech.

Forbes tells Darling that if he wants the licensing laws passed, they have to be consistent with the laws of England.

So Darling holds off for a while longer.

Annual Licence to Publish Newspaper

APPROVAL BY THE GOVERNOR

CAN BE REMOVED AT GOVERNORS DISCRETION*

Governor Darling

*discretion includes if you publish something the governor does not like... especially if it is something mean about the governor.

Meanwhile, two soldiers stationed in Sydney, named Joseph Sudds and Patrick Thompson, decide that life would be much more enjoyable if they get discharged from the army and become convicts. They are not impressed with life in the military and envy the freedom that the convicts seem to enjoy.

With this in mind, they steal some fabrics from a Sydney shopkeeper, intending to be caught. They are convicted of theft and sentenced to seven years transportation to one of the other penal settlements outside of Sydney.

Governor Darling was enraged. He was being made to look the fool!

He had been tasked with making convict transportation something to be genuinely feared, and here were soldiers actively seeking it out! If the life of a convict was so clearly better than the life of a soldier, Darling was failing in his task.

This, at least, was how it would be seen back in England…

So Darling decides to make an example of the pair. He steps in and commutes the sentence, which the Governor had the power to do, but instead of commuting it to something easier or better, he does the opposite and makes it worse.

Now Sudds and Thompson's punishment is to be seven years hard labour in a chain gang, digging and building roads. They are placed in heavy irons, stripped of their uniforms and drummed out of the regiment in a ceremony designed to humiliate and shame them.

What Governor Darling did not know is that Sudds was already seriously ill before this happened.

He would die of fever a few days later in hospital.

Horrified by the treatment of Sudds and Thompson, the Australian newspapers wage a public campaign against Governor Darling, using it as an example of the Governor's behaving like a tyrant, making up his own rules and inflicting cruel and vicious punishments.

The newspaper editors had boasted of the power of the free press to curb unjust government actions. Here was their first real chance to demonstrate that this was happening.

The newspaper campaign succeeds in bringing attention to the situation and holding the Governor to account.

The Australian
Wednesday 13 December 1826

The sentence affords no justification to the employment of unusual chains, or to the infliction of a Military punishment, without a Military trial; but if the sentence of transportation had not been passed neither the double punishment, nor the irons would have been resorted to

…

The Sydney Monitor
Saturday 8 November 1828

A man who goes out of the pale of the law, and evil ensues thereby, is not it seems to plead good intentions. Why depart out of the pale of the law? Is the executor of the laws to take upon him to make new ones, and execute his own laws? If he do do so, he incurs an awful responsibility.

…

The Australian (NSW: 1824-1848), 13 December 1826, page. 3
"THE MONITOR." *The Sydney Monitor (NSW: 1828-1838)*, 08 November 1828, page. 3

Darling is starting to feel attacked. He is supposed to be in power. He is the Governor and it is his job to rule this colony!

The Australian

Tuesday 27 January 1829

We can never believe and affirm that the author and ostensible executor of Sudds' punishment, and which terminated in his death, is a fit person to rule over a British Colony

...

Where would this end? It had started with freedom of the press, but now it is really getting out of control. He decides that it is time to take action.

In April 1827, Governor Darling submits to the Executive Council two draft Bills to control those who run the newspapers and what they can write. One Bill is to impose a stamp duty (tax) on newspapers, another is to regulate newspapers with a licence system.

What would his Chief Justice Francis Forbes say about this?

Dear Governor,

You are going too far. Even if you have originally been instructed by the British government to make this law, the measure itself is 'repugnant to law.' If you are really set on this licence system, you should at least wait until you get the opinion of the British Government's own Law Officers first.

....

Francis Forbes, Chief Justice of NSW)

Dear Governor,

I am not convinced the colony is in immediate danger!! Just because you and the government are being fiercely criticised, (even if it's unfair) does not mean an armed uprising is coming.

AND... If you thought that the colony's peace was so endangered, then why have you waited so long to introduce this Bill?

....

Francis Forbes, Chief Justice of NSW.

Dear Governor,

By the laws of England, the liberty of the press is regarded as a constitutional privilege. This preliminary licence will destroy the freedom of the press and will place it at the discretion of the Government.

....

Francis Forbes, Chief Justice of NSW.

> My dear Judge,
>
> I disagree. The safety of the colony itself is now in danger from the present licentiousness of the press.
>
> .....
>
> The Gov

> My dear Judge,
>
> It is my duty to impose order. It is imperative on me and the well-trained soldier that he should never shirk his duty. I want to pass this bill!
>
> .....
>
> The Gov

Darling is furious.

He thinks that Forbes is causing difficulty where none is needed.

Fictitious letters based on "Governor Darling to Chief Justice Forbes", *Historical Records of Australia*, Series 1, Vol 13, pages. 281-282.

The duty of the Chief Justice of the Supreme Court is to be independent of the Governor.

The Governor is not above the law. He cannot make laws that are unconstitutional and 'repugnant to the laws of England' and then hope to have those laws approved!

....

Francis Forbes, Chief Justice of NSW.

What would they make of it? Which view would win out? The instructions from the British government? Or the principles of checks and balances at the heart of English law?

The Crown Law Officers in London, when they finally received the colonial dispatches and examined the case a year later, declared that Forbes had correctly executed his duty.

Forbes was vindicated.

But Governor Darling never forgave him.

Even though it made Governor Darling angry, Chief Justice Forbes stood firm against the power of Darling to protect the rights of those in the colony.

Extracts from Forbes' Letters

20 September 1827

....

Why have the people of England imposed all these checks and balances? And if they are necessary, why should they be less so in New South Wales?

22 March 1827

....

The judicial office itself stands uncontrolled and independent, and bowing to no power, but the supremacy of the law.

20 September 1827

....

Without other checks in the colony such as trial by jury, the Supreme Court is the only protection against absolute power.

* "Chief Justice Forbes to Under Secretary Horton", 22 March 1827 and 20 September 1827, *Historical Records of Australia*, Series 1, Vol 13 (January 1827- February 1828)

Forbes' ability to remain judicially independent and impartial despite constant pressure from Governor Darling set the foundation for the separation of powers in Australia.

These checks and balances of an independent judiciary and freedom of the press have since become an established part of Australian life.

The rule of law with checks and balances on those in power, is a wonderful protection of individual rights and freedoms to this day.

No-one is above the law

The law is applied equally and fairly

- The law is known and accessible
- Presumption of innocence
- Open justice, independent and impartial judiciary
- No retrospective laws should be made
- Laws are made in an open and transparent way by the people
- Government agencies to behave as model litigants
- Fair and prompt trials
- Separation of powers between Legislature Executive Judiciary
- People can only be punished in accordance with the law
- The law and its administration is subject to open and free criticism

Checks and Balances and the Rule of Law

Under the rule of law, everyone is entitled to the protection of the law, regardless of their status. This book demonstrates the need for checks and balances to prevent those in authority from abusing their power. An independent judiciary that is free from external pressure can dispense justice to all individuals according to the law. Additionally, a free press that can criticise government actions is an essential safeguard that enhances accountability and protects the rights of the community.

The Rule of Law Education Centre educates and informs school students about how the Magna Carta and subsequent rule of law principles have impacted and contributed to the history, culture and legal processes of Australia. It endeavours to strengthen the rule of law and human rights through education.

For more information, including additional education resources and how you can support our work go to www.ruleoflaw.org.au

> Wentworth and Forbes were made of stern and independent stuff and intended to make their voices heard. Thus began a line of independent strong-minded Australians who defended the freedom of press and an independent judiciary with all their strength.
>
> – Robin Speed OAM

www.ruleoflaw.org.au | info@ruleoflaw.org.au

Copyright © 2024 All rights reserved.